THE

BEAUTY

OF

ITALY

Italy, officially the **Italian Republic** (Italian: *Repubblica Italiana* [re ˈpubblika itaˈljaːna]), is a European country consisting of a peninsula delimited by the Italian Alps and surrounded by several islands. Located in the middle of the Mediterranean sea and traversed along its length by the Apennines, Italy has a largely temperate seasonal climate. The country covers an area of 301,340 km2 (116,350 sq mi) and shares open land borders with France, Slovenia, Austria, Switzerland and the enclaved microstates of Vatican City and San Marino. Italy has a territorial exclave in Switzerland (Campione) and a maritime exclave in the Tunisian sea (Lampedusa). With around 60 million inhabitants, Italy is the fourth-most populous member state of the European Union.

Due to its central geographic location in Southern Europe and the Mediterranean, Italy has historically been home to a myriad of peoples and cultures. In addition to the various ancient peoples dispersed throughout modern-day Italy, the most predominant being the Indo-European Italic peoples who gave the peninsula its name, beginning from the classical era, Phoenicians and Carthaginiansfounded colonies in insular Italy, Greeks established settlements in the so-called *Magna Graecia* of southern Italy, while Etruscansand Celts inhabited central and northern Italy respectively. The Italic tribe known as the Latins formed the Roman Kingdom in the 8th century BC, which eventually became a republic with a government of the Senate and the People. The Roman Republic conqueredand assimilated its neighbours on the peninsula, in some cases through the establishment of federations, and the Republic eventually expanded and conquered parts of Europe, North Africa and the Middle East. By the first century BC, the Roman Empireemerged as the dominant power in the Mediterranean Basin and became the leading cultural, political and religious centre of Western civilisation, inaugurating the Pax Romana, a period of more than 200 years during which Italy's technology, economy, artand literature flourished. Italy remained the homeland of the Romans and the metropole of the Roman Empire. The legacy of the Roman Empire endured its fall and can be observed in the global distribution of culture, law, governments, Christianity and the Latin script.

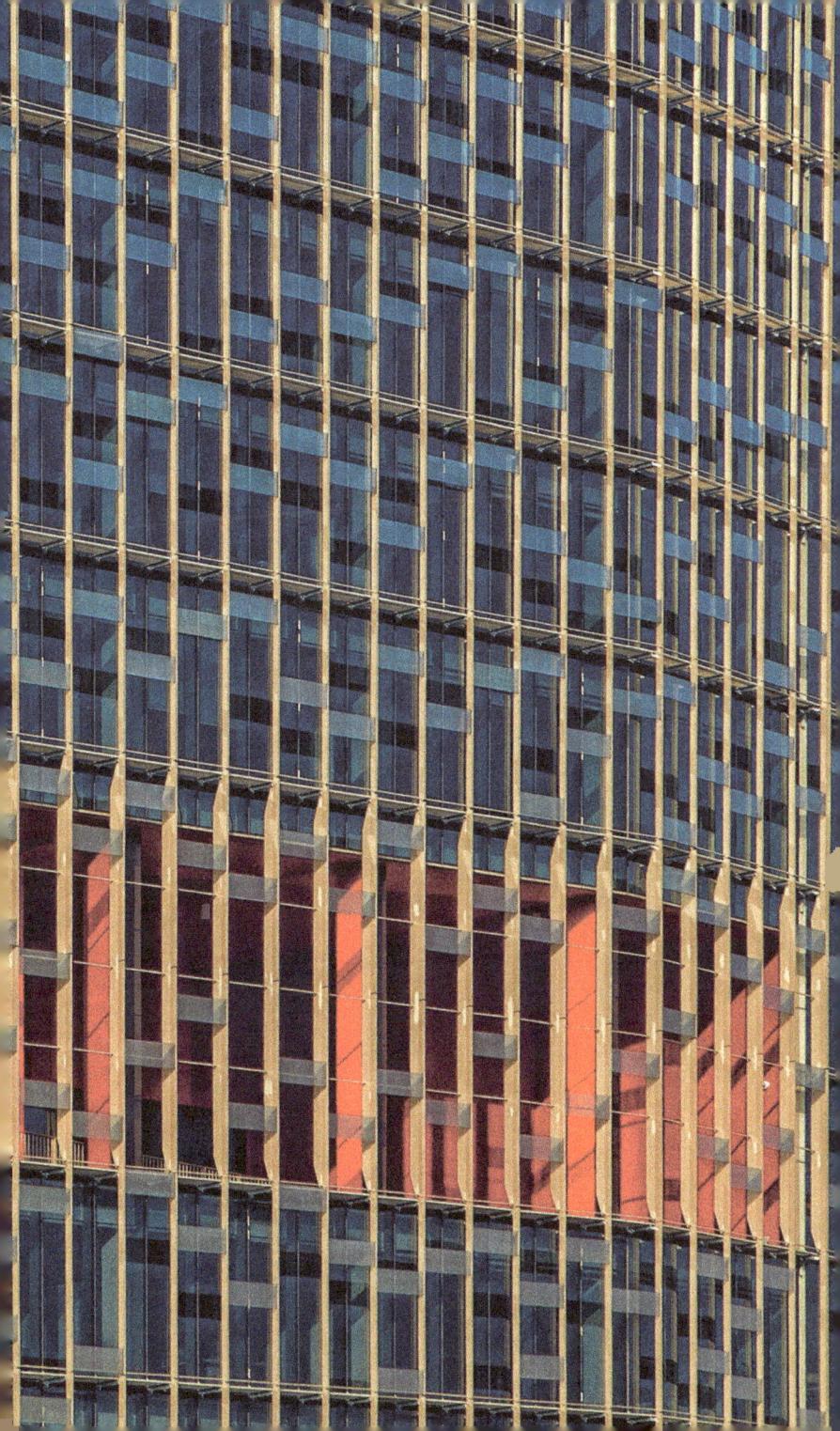